Manuscript Handwriting

Editor: Carla Hamaguchi
Illustrator: Darcy Tom
Designer/Production: Moonhee Pak/Terri Lamadrid
Cover Designer: Barbara Peterson
Art Director: Tom Cochrane
Project Director: Carolea Williams

Table of Contents

Introduction

Each book in the *Power Practice*™ series contains dozens of ready-to-use activity pages to provide students with skill practice. The fun activities can be used to supplement and enhance what you are already teaching in your classroom. Give an activity page to students as independent class work, or send the pages home as homework to reinforce skills taught in class. An answer key is provided for quick reference for pages that require a specific answer.

The activity pages in *Traditional Manuscript Handwriting* provide the perfect practice for enhancing students' handwriting. The practical and creative activities provide students with practice in recognizing and forming capital and lowercase letters. As students complete the activities, they will improve their handwriting as well as practice these skills:
- letter sounds
- rhyming words
- counting syllables
- sight word recognition
- alphabetical order
- word categorization
- sentence formation

Use these ready-to-go activities to "recharge" skill review and give students the power to succeed!

The Alphabet

Aa Bb Cc Dd

Ee Ff Gg Hh

Ii Jj Kk Ll

Mm Nn Oo Pp

Qq Rr Ss Tt

Uu Vv Ww Xx

Yy Zz

ABC

Capital Letters

A   B   C   D

E   F   G   H

I   J   K   L

M   N   O   P

Q   R   S   T

U   V   W   X

Y   Z

ABCs

Traditional Manuscript Handwriting © 2004 Creative Teaching Press

Lowercase Letters

a   b   c   d

e   f   g   h

i   j   k   l

m   n   o   p

q   r   s   t

u   v   w   x

y   z

Missing Letters

A__   B b   __ c   D __

E __   __ f   G g   __ h

I __   J j   __ k   L l

__ m   N __   O o   __ p

Q __   __ r   S s   T __

U u   V __   __ w   X __

Y __   __ z

A

A

A

A

A

A

Albert

Alaska

My very best

Name _____

a 🍎

a

a

a

My very best _ _ _ _ _ _

Draw something that starts with the letter **a**.

Traditional Manuscript Handwriting © 2004 Creative Teaching Press

Name _____

B

B

B

B

B

B

Beth

Brazil

My very best

Name _____

b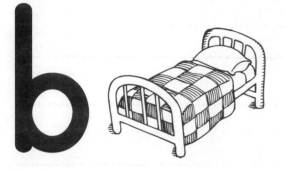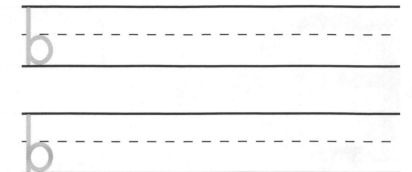

b

b

b

b

Draw something that starts with the letter **b**.

Traditional Manuscript Handwriting © 2004 Creative Teaching Press

Name _____

C  C C -

C C -

C -

C C -

C -

Carson

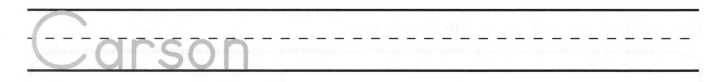

Colorado

My very best

Name _____

C

c

c

c

c

My very best

Draw something that starts with the letter **c**.

Traditional Manuscript Handwriting © 2004 Creative Teaching Press

Name _____

D

D

D

D

Denise

Delaware

My very best

Name _____

d

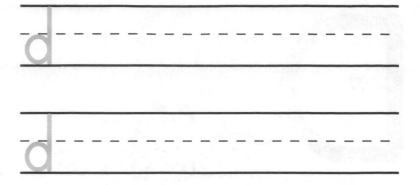

d

d

d

d

Draw something that starts with the letter **d**.

Traditional Manuscript Handwriting © 2004 Creative Teaching Press

E

E

E

E

E

E

Edward

Egypt

Traditional Manuscript Handwriting © 2004 Creative Teaching Press

Name _____

e

_____
- - - - - - - - - - - - - - - - -
e
_____

_____
e
_____

_____
e
- - - - - - - - - - - - - - - - -
_____

_____
e
- - - - - - - - - - - - - - - - -
_____

My very best

_____
- - - - - - - - -
_____

Draw something that starts with the letter **e**.

Traditional Manuscript Handwriting © 2004 Creative Teaching Press

Name _____

F 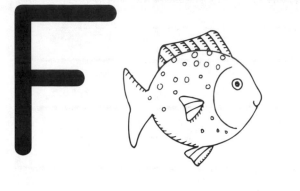 F

F

F

F

Faith

Florida

My very best

Traditional Manuscript Handwriting © 2004 Creative Teaching Press

Name _____

f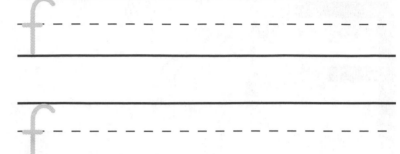

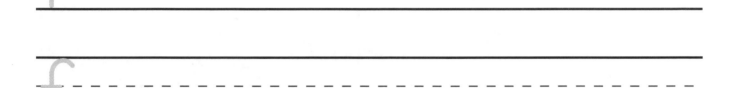

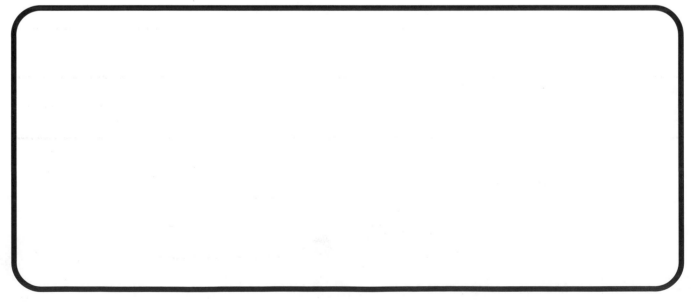

Draw something that starts with the letter **f**.

Traditional Manuscript Handwriting © 2004 Creative Teaching Press

My very best

Name _____

g

g

g

g

g

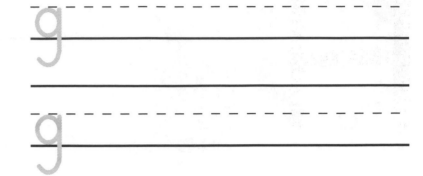

Draw something that starts with the letter **g**.

Traditional Manuscript Handwriting © 2004 Creative Teaching Press

Name _____

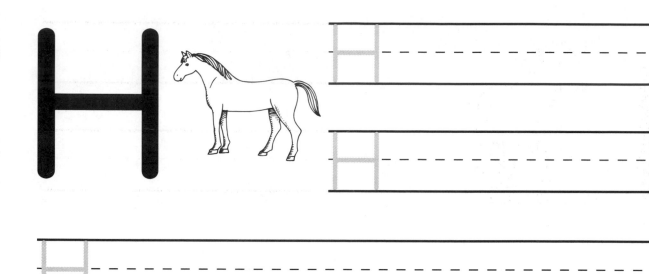

H

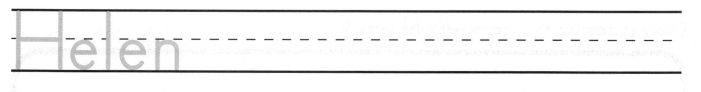

H

H

Helen

Hawaii

My very best

Traditional Manuscript Handwriting © 2004 Creative Teaching Press

Name _____

h

h

h

h

Draw something that starts with the letter **h**.

Name _____

I

I

I

I

I

I

Ian

Israel

My very best

i

My very best _____

Draw something that starts with the letter i.

Traditional Manuscript Handwriting © 2004 Creative Teaching Press

Name _____

J

J J -------------------------------

J J -------------------------------

J J -------------------------------

J J -------------------------------

J J -------------------------------

Janet -------------------------------

Japan

My very best

Traditional Manuscript Handwriting © 2004 Creative Teaching Press

Name _____

j

j   j   j

j

j

Draw something that starts with the letter **j**.

Traditional Manuscript Handwriting © 2004 Creative Teaching Press

Name _____

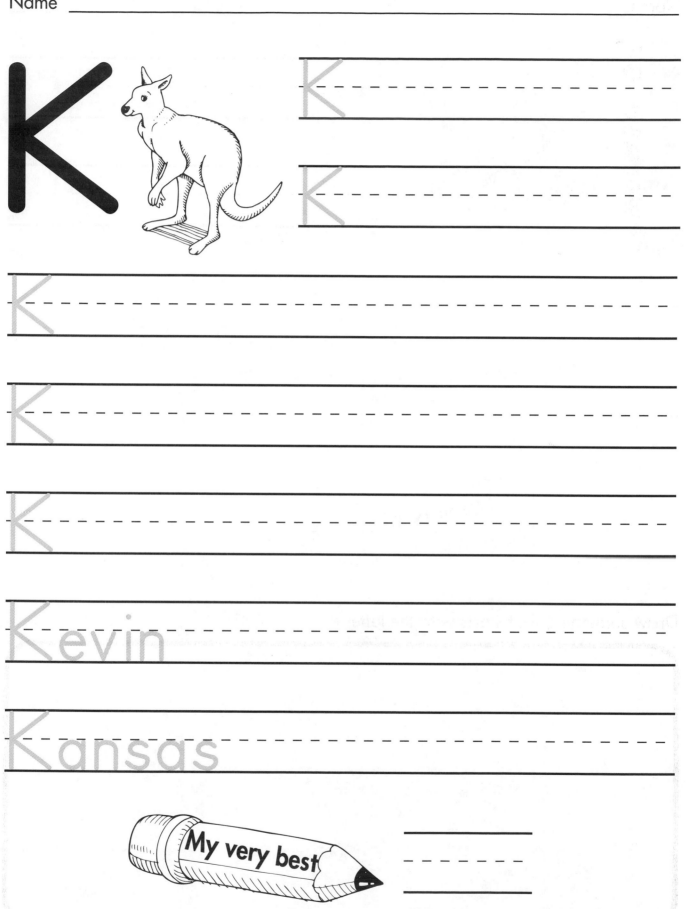

Kevin

Kansas

My very best

Draw something that starts with the letter **k**.

Traditional Manuscript Handwriting © 2004 Creative Teaching Press

L

Linda

Louisiana

My very best

Traditional Manuscript Handwriting © 2004 Creative Teaching Press

Name _____

My very best

Draw something that starts with the letter l.

Traditional Manuscript Handwriting © 2004 Creative Teaching Press

Name _____

M  M M -------------------------------

M M -------------------------------

M ---

M ---

M ---

Marcus

Montana

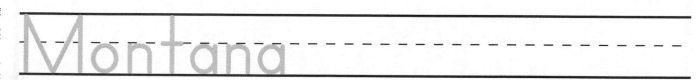
My very best

Traditional Manuscript Handwriting © 2004 Creative Teaching Press

Name _____

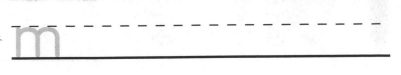

m

m

My very best

Draw something that starts with the letter **m**.

Traditional Manuscript Handwriting © 2004 Creative Teaching Press

Nancy

Nevada

My very best

Traditional Manuscript Handwriting © 2004 Creative Teaching Press

Name _____

n

    n

    n

n

n

My very best

Draw something that starts with the letter **n**.

Traditional Manuscript Handwriting © 2004 Creative Teaching Press

Name

Omar

Oklahoma

My very best

Name _____

O o

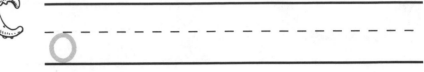

o

o

Draw something that starts with the letter **o**.

Traditional Manuscript Handwriting © 2004 Creative Teaching Press

Name _____

P

P   P -

P   P -

P -

P -

P -

Penny -

Paris -

My very best

Name _____

p

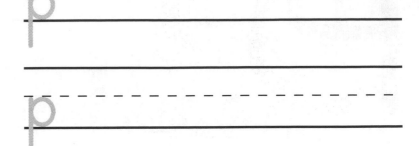

p

p

p

p

My very best _____

Draw something that starts with the letter **p**.

Traditional Manuscript Handwriting © 2004 Creative Teaching Press

Name _____

Q

Q

Q

Q

Queen

Quebec

My very best

Traditional Manuscript Handwriting © 2004 Creative Teaching Press

Name _____

q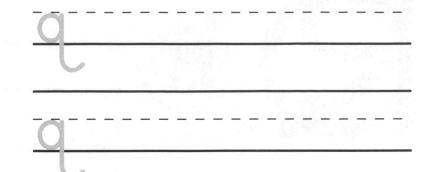

q

q

q

q

Draw something that starts with the letter **q**.

Traditional Manuscript Handwriting © 2004 Creative Teaching Press

R

R R -----------------

R R -----------------

R -------------------------------

R -------------------------------

R -------------------------------

Robert -------------------------

Rome -----------------------------

My very best

Name _____

r

r

r

r

r

My very best

Draw something that starts with the letter **r**.

Traditional Manuscript Handwriting © 2004 Creative Teaching Press

Name _____

S 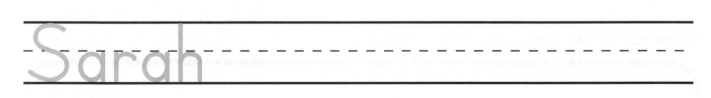 S

S

S

S

S

Sarah

Sweden

My very best ___

Traditional Manuscript Handwriting © 2004 Creative Teaching Press

Name _____

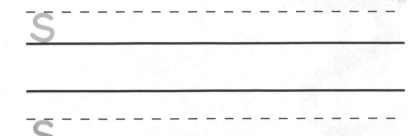

s

s

s

s

Draw something that starts with the letter **s**.

Traditional Manuscript Handwriting © 2004 Creative Teaching Press

T    T

T

T

T

Tyler

Toronto

Name _____

My very best

Draw something that starts with the letter **t**.

Traditional Manuscript Handwriting © 2004 Creative Teaching Press

U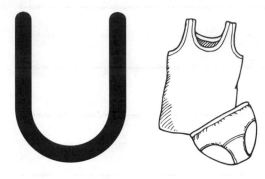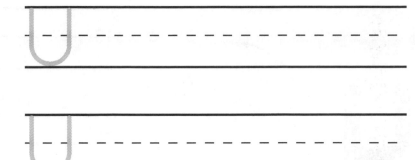

U

U

Ursula

Utah

Traditional Manuscript Handwriting © 2004 Creative Teaching Press

Name _____

u

u ‑ ‑ ‑ ‑ ‑ ‑ ‑ ‑ ‑ ‑ ‑ ‑ ‑ ‑ ‑ ‑

u ‑ ‑ ‑ ‑ ‑ ‑ ‑ ‑ ‑ ‑ ‑ ‑ ‑ ‑ ‑ ‑

u ‑ ‑ ‑ ‑ ‑ ‑ ‑ ‑ ‑ ‑ ‑ ‑ ‑ ‑ ‑ ‑

u ‑ ‑ ‑ ‑ ‑ ‑ ‑ ‑ ‑ ‑ ‑ ‑ ‑ ‑ ‑ ‑

My very best

Draw something that starts with the letter **u**.

Traditional Manuscript Handwriting © 2004 Creative Teaching Press

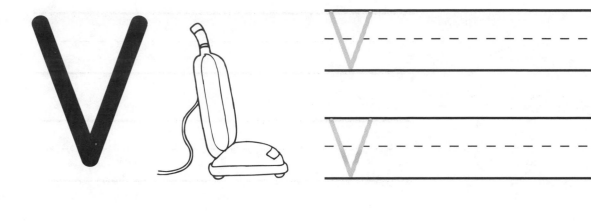

V

V
V

V

V

V

Victor

Vermont

My very best

Traditional Manuscript Handwriting © 2004 Creative Teaching Press

Name _____

V

_____
V - - - - - - - - - - - - - - - - -
_____
V - - - - - - - - - - - - - - - - -

V -

V -

My very best
_____
- - - - -
_____

Draw something that starts with the letter **v**.

 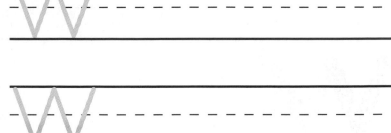

W   w

W

W

W

W

Wendy

Wyoming

 My very best

Traditional Manuscript Handwriting © 2004 Creative Teaching Press

Name _____

W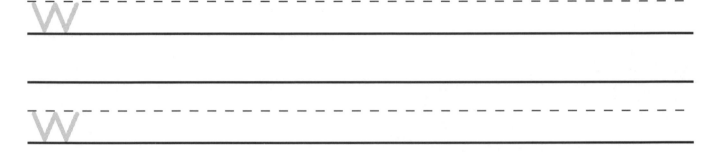

W

W

W

W

Draw something that starts with the letter **w**.

X

Xavier

Xerox

My very best _____

Name _____

X

x

X

X

My very best

Draw something that starts with the letter **x**.

Traditional Manuscript Handwriting © 2004 Creative Teaching Press

Name _____

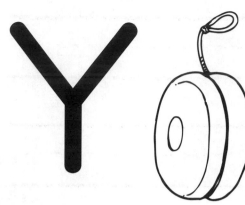

Y

Y

Y

Y

Yolanda

Yemen

My very best

Traditional Manuscript Handwriting © 2004 Creative Teaching Press

Name _____

y

y

y

y

y

My very best

Draw something that starts with the letter **y**.

Traditional Manuscript Handwriting © 2004 Creative Teaching Press

Name _____

Z

Z ‑

Z ‑

Z ‑

Z ‑

Z ‑

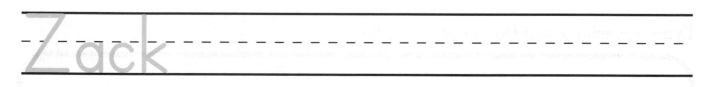

Zack ‑

Zaire ‑

My very best

Name _____

z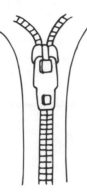

z

z

z

z

Draw something that starts with the letter **z**.

Traditional Manuscript Handwriting © 2004 Creative Teaching Press

My Very Best Capital Letters

A B C D E F G H I J K L M N O P Q R S T U V W X Y Z

Write each capital letter in your very best writing.

My Very Best Lowercase Letters

a b c d e f g h i j k l m n o p q r s t u v w x y z

Write each lowercase letter in your very best writing.

Traditional Manuscript Handwriting © 2004 Creative Teaching Press

A–C Words

apple

airplane

brain

butterfly

camera

cookie

Traditional Manuscript Handwriting © 2004 Creative Teaching Press

D–F Words

drawing

dresser

eraser

elephant

flamingo

feather

Traditional Manuscript Handwriting © 2004 Creative Teaching Press

G–I Words

goose

garden

hammer

homework

inside

imagine

Traditional Manuscript Handwriting © 2004 Creative Teaching Press

J–L Words

jaguar

judge

kangaroo

king

lemon

library

M–O Words

mouse

minute

night

neighbor

olive

octopus

P–R Words

park

parade

queen

quiet

rainbow

rabbit

S–U Words

school

shark

tooth

turkey

umbrella

unicorn

V–X Words

vase

violin

window

water

x-ray

xylophone

Traditional Manuscript Handwriting © 2004 Creative Teaching Press

Y–Z Words

year

youth

yesterday

zebra

zipper

zero

Traditional Manuscript Handwriting © 2004 Creative Teaching Press

Colors

red

blue

yellow

green

orange

purple

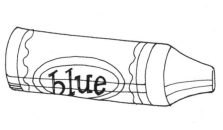
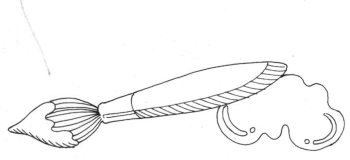

Colors

black

brown

white

pink

gray

magenta

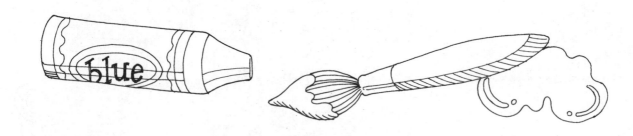

Shapes

◯ <u>circle</u> - - - - - - - - - - - - -

□ <u>square</u>

△ <u>triangle</u> - - - - - - - - - - -

▭ <u>rectangle</u> - - - - - - - - -

◯ <u>oval</u> - - - - - - - - - - - - - - - -

◇ <u>diamond</u> - - - - - - - - - -

Numbers

1 one

2 two

3 three

4 four

5 five

Numbers

6 six

7 seven

8 eight

9 nine

10 ten

Traditional Manuscript Handwriting © 2004 Creative Teaching Press

Numbers

11
eleven

12
twelve

13
thirteen

14
fourteen

15
fifteen

Numbers

16
sixteen

17
seventeen

18
eighteen

19
nineteen

20
twenty

Traditional Manuscript Handwriting © 2004 Creative Teaching Press

Numbers

21
twenty-one

22
twenty-two

23
twenty-three

24
twenty-four

25
twenty-five

Numbers

26
twenty-six

27
twenty-seven

28
twenty-eight

29
twenty-nine

30
thirty

Ordinal Numbers

1st
2nd
3rd
4th
5th
6th

 first

 second

 third

 fourth

 fifth

 sixth

Traditional Manuscript Handwriting © 2004 Creative Teaching Press

Name _____

Money

 cent

 penny

 nickel

 dime

 quarter

 dollar

Traditional Manuscript Handwriting © 2004 Creative Teaching Press

Days of the Week

Sunday

Monday

Tuesday

Wednesday

Thursday

Friday

Saturday

Name _____

Months of the Year

January

February

March

April

May

June

Traditional Manuscript Handwriting © 2004 Creative Teaching Press

Months of the Year

July

August

September

October

November

December

Traditional Manuscript Handwriting © 2004 Creative Teaching Press

Name _____

Weather Words

sunny

rainy

snowy

overcast

foggy

windy

Traditional Manuscript Handwriting © 2004 Creative Teaching Press

Name _____

Seasons and Holidays

winter

spring

summer

fall

Easter

Hanukkah

Flag Day

winter   spring   summer   fall

Traditional Manuscript Handwriting © 2004 Creative Teaching Press

Holidays

July 4th

Halloween

Thanksgiving

Christmas

St. Patrick's Day

Traditional Manuscript Handwriting © 2004 Creative Teaching Press

Name _____

Directional Words

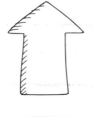 up

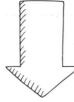 down

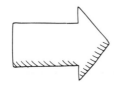 right

 left

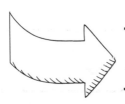 under

 over

What a Family!

mother --------------------------------

father --------------------------------

sister --------------------------------

brother --------------------------------

aunt --------------------------------

uncle --------------------------------

Traditional Manuscript Handwriting © 2004 Creative Teaching Press

School Subjects

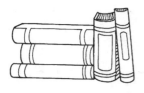 reading

 writing

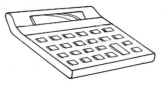 math

 science

 art

 social studies

School Supplies

pencil

paper

stapler

books

crayons

scissors

ruler

Traditional Manuscript Handwriting © 2004 Creative Teaching Press

Good Work Words

great

nice

super

wow

good

excellent

terrific

Traditional Manuscript Handwriting © 2004 Creative Teaching Press

Name _____

Body Parts

head

eye

arm

foot

hand

ear

nose

leg

Write each body part.

_____   _____

- - - - - - - - - - - -   - - - - - - - - - - - -

_____   _____

- - - - - - - - - - - -   - - - - - - - - - - - -

_____   _____

- - - - - - - - - - - -   - - - - - - - - - - - -

_____   _____

- - - - - - - - - - - -   - - - - - - - - - - - -

_____   _____

Traditional Manuscript Handwriting © 2004 Creative Teaching Press

Name _____

Careers

doctor

teacher

artist

farmer

dancer

pilot

author

Sight Words

the

to

and

he

you

it

of

Traditional Manuscript Handwriting © 2004 Creative Teaching Press

Sight Words

in

was

said

his

that

she

for

Sight Words

on

they

but

had

at

him

with

Traditional Manuscript Handwriting © 2004 Creative Teaching Press

Sight Words

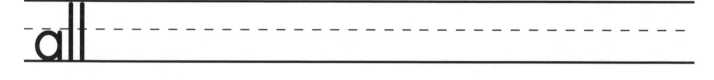

up

all

look

is

her

there

some

Sight Words

out

as

be

have

go

we

am

Traditional Manuscript Handwriting © 2004 Creative Teaching Press

Sight Words

then

little

down

do

can

could

when

Name _____

Sight Words

did

what

so

see

not

were

like

Traditional Manuscript Handwriting © 2004 Creative Teaching Press

-at Word Family

Write each word.

| bat | fat | cat | hat | sat | mat |

_____   _____
- - - - - - - - - - - - -   - - - - - - - - - - - - -
_____   _____

_____   _____
- - - - - - - - - - - - -   - - - - - - - - - - - - -
_____   _____

_____   _____
- - - - - - - - - - - - -   - - - - - - - - - - - - -
_____   _____

Write the sentence.

The fat cat sat on the mat.

_____
- -
_____

_____
- -
_____

Name _____

-et Word Family

Write each word.

| jet | get | let | met | net | pet |

Write the sentence.

He let the pet get in the net.

Traditional Manuscript Handwriting © 2004 Creative Teaching Press

-ig Word Family

Write each word.

big	dig	pig	rig	wig	fig

Write the sentence.

The pig wore a big wig.

-og Word Family

Write each word.

| dog | hog | jog | log | frog | fog |

Write the sentence.

The dog and frog sat on a log.

-un Word Family

Write each word.

| fun | run | sun | bun | nun | spun |

_____   _____

- - - - - - - - - - - - - -   - - - - - - - - - - - - - -

_____   _____

_____   _____

- - - - - - - - - - - - - -   - - - - - - - - - - - - - -

_____   _____

_____   _____

- - - - - - - - - - - - - -   - - - - - - - - - - - - - -

_____   _____

Write the sentence.

The nun had fun in the sun.

_____

- -

_____

_____

- -

_____

Alphabetical Order—Food

Write the words in alphabetical order on the lines below.

| corn | lettuce | squash | peas | onion | tomato |

Alphabetical Order—Ocean

Write the words in alphabetical order on the lines below.

| crab | fish | shell | whale | eel | lobster |

_____

- -

_____

- -

_____

- -

_____

- -

_____

- -

_____

- -

_____

Alphabetical Order—Zoo

Write the words in alphabetical order on the lines below.

snake   bear   monkey   giraffe   lion   tiger

Traditional Manuscript Handwriting © 2004 Creative Teaching Press

Rhyming Words

Write the rhyming words next to each other on the lines below.

car	moon	rat	star	skunk
chair	spoon	bear	hat	trunk

_____ _____

_____ _____

_____ _____

_____ _____

_____ _____

Rhyming Words

Write the rhyming words next to each other on the lines below.

key	pick	bug	bee	pie
dog	rug	cry	stick	frog

_____

_ _ _ _ _ _ _ _ _ _ _ _ _ _ _

_____

_ _ _ _ _ _ _ _ _ _ _ _ _ _ _

_____

_ _ _ _ _ _ _ _ _ _ _ _ _ _ _

_____

_ _ _ _ _ _ _ _ _ _ _ _ _ _ _

_____

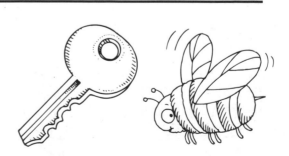

Rhyming Words

Write the rhyming words next to each other on the lines below.

cake	fan	pen	snake	duck
sled	man	ten	bed	truck

_____   _____

- - - - - - - - - - - - - - - -   - - - - - - - - - - - - - - - -

_____   _____

- - - - - - - - - - - - - - - -   - - - - - - - - - - - - - - - -

_____   _____

- - - - - - - - - - - - - - - -   - - - - - - - - - - - - - - - -

_____   _____

- - - - - - - - - - - - - - - -   - - - - - - - - - - - - - - - -

_____   _____

- - - - - - - - - - - - - - - -   - - - - - - - - - - - - - - - -

_____   _____

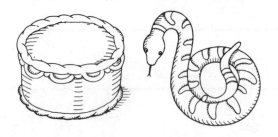
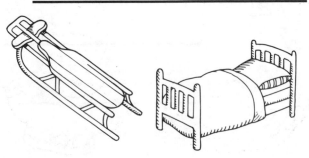

What Am I?

Write each word next to its matching picture.

| cat | sun | boat | foot | house | table |

What Am I?

Write each word next to its matching picture.

tree	goat	cake	bus	kite	fish

Name _____

Syllables

Write each word under the correct category.

one	very	yes	color	pig
happy	pretty	ball	people	blue

One Syllable	Two Syllables

Name _____

Categorize

Write each word under the correct category.

dog	corn	pizza	monkey	eggs
bear	pig	goat	peas	bread

Food	Animals
_____	_____
- - - - - - - - -	- - - - - - - - -
_____	_____
- - - - - - - - -	- - - - - - - - -
_____	_____
- - - - - - - - -	- - - - - - - - -
_____	_____
- - - - - - - - -	- - - - - - - - -
_____	_____

Categorize

Write each word under the correct category.

rain	eat	tree	cup	sock
pot	ring	bat	name	pet

3-Letter Words	4-Letter Words

Traditional Manuscript Handwriting © 2004 Creative Teaching Press

Name _____

Put It in Order

Put the circles in numerical order. Write each word in order to make a sentence.

 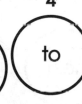   

3 — a   2 — is   4 — pig.   1 — This

_____
- - - - - - - - - - - - - - - -
_____
- - - - - - - - - - - - - - - -
_____

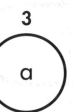 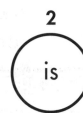   

5 — sit.   1 — My   4 — to   2 — dog   3 — likes

_____
- - - - - - - - - - - - - - - -
_____
- - - - - - - - - - - - - - - -
_____

Put It in Order

Put the circles in numerical order. Write each word in order to make a sentence.

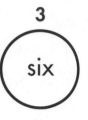 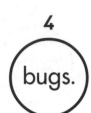 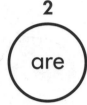 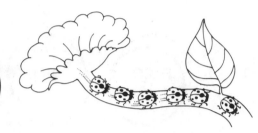

3	4	2	1
six	bugs.	are	There

- - - - - - - - - - - - - - - - - -

- - - - - - - - - - - - - - - - - -

3	1	5	2	4	6
is	The	a	bird	in	nest.

- - - - - - - - - - - - - - - - - -

- - - - - - - - - - - - - - - - - -

Traditional Manuscript Handwriting © 2004 Creative Teaching Press

Put It in Order

Put the circles in numerical order. Write each word in order to make a sentence.

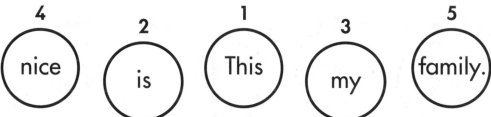

4 **nice** 2 **is** 1 **This** 3 **my** 5 **family.**

_____

- - - - - - - - - - - - - - - -

_____

- - - - - - - - - - - - - - - -

_____

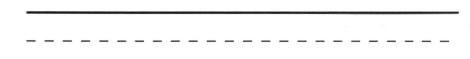

4 **I** 2 **dad** 7 **the** 1 **My** 6 **to** 3 **and** 5 **went** 8 **zoo.**

_____

- - - - - - - - - - - - - - - -

_____

- - - - - - - - - - - - - - - -

_____

Name _____

Sentence Mix-Up

Pick a phrase from each box to create a sentence. Write each sentence on the blank lines below.

The boy went to	the market.
The girl ran to	school.
The man is at	the park.

Traditional Manuscript Handwriting © 2004 Creative Teaching Press

Sentence Mix-Up

Pick a phrase from each box to create a sentence. Write each sentence on the blank lines below.

| The cat slept
I sat
My computer is | on a chair.
on my desk.
on the rug. |

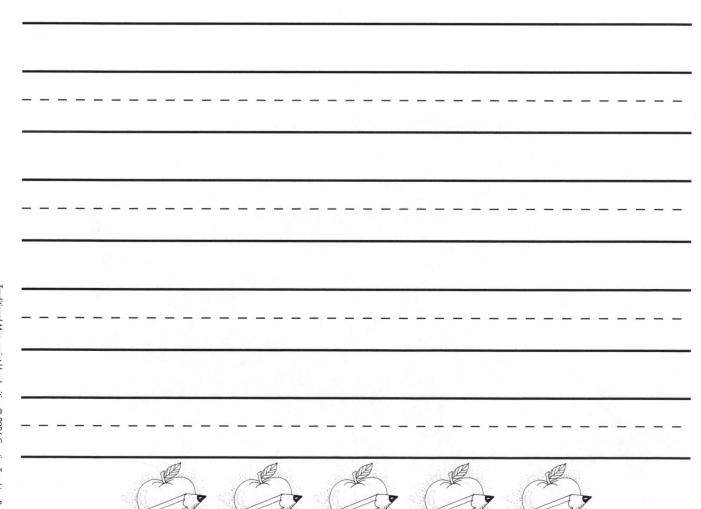

Sentence Mix-Up

Pick a phrase from each box to create a sentence. Write each sentence on the blank lines below.

The lion is	hungry.
John's bird is	loud.
The baby was	crying.

Traditional Manuscript Handwriting © 2004 Creative Teaching Press

Sentence Mix-Up

Pick a phrase from each box to create a sentence. Write each sentence on the blank lines below.

I have a This is my He has a	toy. brother. pet.

Traditional Manuscript Handwriting © 2004 Creative Teaching Press

Name _____

All About Me

My name is
_____
- -
_____ .

I'm _____ years old.

My birthday is
_____
- -
_____ .

I'm in the _____ grade.

All About Me

My favorite color is

_____
- -
_____ .

My friends' names are

_____
- -
_____ .

My address is

_____
- -
_____ .

My phone number is

_____
- -
_____ .

Answer Key

Alphabetical Order (page 108)

Food

corn

lettuce

onion

peas

squash

tomato

Alphabetical Order (page 109)

Ocean

crab

eel

fish

lobster

shell

whale

Alphabetical Order (page 110)

Zoo

bear

giraffe

lion

monkey

snake

tiger

Rhyming Words (page 111)

car—star

bear—chair

moon—spoon

rat—hat

trunk—skunk

Rhyming Words (page 112)

key—bee

pick—stick

frog—dog

bug—rug

cry—pie

Rhyming Words (page 113)

cake—snake

fan—man

bed—sled

truck—duck

pen—ten

What Am I? (page 114)

cat

table

boat

foot

house

sun

What Am I? (page 115)

bus

tree

fish

kite

goat

cake

Syllables (page 116)

One Syllable

one

yes

pig

ball

blue

Two Syllables

very

color

happy

pretty

people

Categorize (page 117)

Food

corn

pizza

eggs

peas

bread

Animals

dog

bear

pig

goat

monkey

Categorize (page 118)

3-Letter Words

eat

cup

pot

bat

pet

4-Letter Words

rain

tree

sock

ring

name

Put It in Order (page 119)

This is a pig.

My dog likes to sit.

Put It in Order (page 120)

There are six bugs.

The bird is in a nest.

Put It in Order (page 121)

This is my nice family.

My dad and I went to the zoo.